GRADIENTS AND FERVOURS

AMULYA ANIL

Made with ♥ on the Notion Press Platform
www.notionpress.com

For everything that breathes life into Earth

Contents

Contents

Acknowledgements

For those who have helped me experience the intricacies of life, Thank You.

From The Author's Desk

And in the next few pages are some words which found me.

Love,

Amulya Anil

Prologue

Thoughts have an ocean of their own.

Even if you put some on the paper, for the world to cherish,

The Ocean would still remain.

1. Snowman

Everything seemed right,
Though it was all just white.
He stood at the peak of his might,
While I watched him all night.
A muffler or two, I would clad him with.
And googly eyes to ensure he's no myth.
Spent many breaths on him,
And for his well-being, chanted a hymn.
In dilemma I now wonder,
To be cold or not to be, I ponder.
For my warmth caused his decay,
He was a snowman who melted away.

2. Semper Fortis

A stormy night, or the feeble wind,
There's a man who hopes to find,
A ray of white, amidst the walls of black,
That might sneak in through a tiny crack.
From a heart full of love, flows the valour.
And where there is faith, stays all the color.
"No fear of fear", he says,
The sun sets only once, all the days.
the even exists only between the odds.....

3. Paused

The tress wouldn't stand still
And the mountains would grow.
The clouds would spill
And the rivers could flow.
Some days, they bowed down to time,
And on the others, time paused to find its rhyme.
Then the tree would stand still,
And the mountains wouldn't grow.
The clouds wouldn't spilll
And the rivers couldn't flow.
For to just bend,
Is never to end.

4. Life Still Goes On

That morning, I remember, was of haze.
I plucked a flower hoping that it stays.
On my table, in a tumbler, and at it I would gaze.
When the sun set, I cringed, we took the different ways.
The flower withered away,no more hue.
Not the same anymore, I knew.
But the next morning, I plucked another.
Life still goes on and there's not much to bother.

5. The Maple Tree

The Maple Tree I once knew,
Evolved greens to browns.
Witnessed smiles and frowns,
Little by little, striving to be anew.
Through the days, inch by inch it grows,
Time would roll, yet the world still glows.
Another year has gone by, the maple is older,
The seeds it dispered would though be bolder.
As I see much of the maple tree,
Subtle things of existence, I discover.
That the life in hand never comes for free,
It costs time, for all that is to endeavor.

6. Being Close

Not all of them who are beside you, are close to you,
And not all of them who are close to you are beside you.

7. Never in the Dark

He asked me if I would light a candle for him,
If he were no longer alive.
But, I would continue to glow for him,
The light I would never deprive.

8. Memories

My memories are wrinkled the way you and I are.
When the night falls, it allows the dew drops to settle on them
And then, the memories too age with us.

9. Love and Smiles

Love was never just about him holding on to my smiles,
But also about allowing him to hold on to his smiles.

10. Rain Drops

I wait for the rain drops to beckon.
Sometimes to hide my tears.
And sometimes, to wash the sin,
Off my skin.

11. The Moon and the Sun

The Moon is a million years younger,
The Sun still shares his light.
The Sun is a million years away,
The Moon still knows his might.
The Moon and the Sun,
Are never out of each other's sight.

12. Storming

Our relationship was that of the wind and the sail.
I wandered in the direction he travelled in.
But now, I'm an entire storm myself.

13. Fear of the Known

Plains not any woods, yet lost.
I seek myself the most.
From realties to fairytales, I sway.
Amidst which I seek a way.
The feet of my own,
But the path unknown.
The fear of the known engulfs me more,
Than that of an unknown door.

14. Finding Yourself

Everything that you lost
In the process of finding yourself,
will find its way back to you
before it loses itself.

15. Independency

Growing up makes you realise that independency is a myth. The world runs on mutual reliability and no one is really on his own.

16. Blind

It was never that the world is colourless,
But the man who is blind.

17. Sunrises and Us

We know that the sun rises and sets everday,
But lights up the sky and darkens it differently, each time.
Perhaps, that's how even we humans are.

18. Spring

You remind me of the *spring*.

The way you can convert almost nothing into something more with life.

19. Northern Lights

He's like the northern lights,
You wouldn't find everywhere.
But when you do, you would pause to just watch him glow,
As though his aura lit up an entire universe.

20. Your Seasons

I know your seasons.
Scorching summers to shivering winters,
And all that in between.
Thunderstorms and hailstones.
I know your seasons well enough for us to be.

21. Memories of You

Somewhere between blue skies
And white clouds , thd green grass and browns.
I hold the memories of you.

22. Hope

The abandoned waters or a sprinting river,
A hot spring or even an entire ocean,
You are the hope who stays afloat.

23. You and the Dark

You would ask me to find you in the dark. But, trust me, if you were there, then it would indeed be everything but dark.

24. Building Constellations

You and I are scattered pieces of glowing dust.
If we were to pause and look at each other,
We woud build an entire constellation.

25. Half of Us

Like the moon, the half you is lit while the other half isn't.

We all belong to the moon, one way or the other.

26. You

You are a story with a conclusion which no one knows.

27. Nights

The night does not stay long before the day takes over. But it stays long enough to tell us - that the moon is not a while every night, nevertheless he still glows.

28. Tornado

The wind keeps whistling. You might find a tornado in yourself once in a while.

29. Darkness and Otherwise

Darkness beckons, we have mornings to catch some light.
When the nights blind, you and I have the night.
Sun-catchers and then the dream catchers - we play,
Planet earth rotates slowly, we shall always find a way.

30. Story

If life were to *show* me a story, it would be **you**.

31. Days and Shadows

The nights show me more light than the days do,
For the days are more of shadows.

32. Between Life and Death

Between life and death,

There's a distance you and I do not know.

And you bridge it well, for me.

33. Shores from the Shores

We look at the shores from the shores.
You know, it wasn't the seas in between,
But the fact that we did not want to swim across.

34. Rainbows of Life

You color me not merely skin deep,
But in a thousand better ways than anyone else could.
For sailing through the pacific and sharing the hue of your soul, vibrant enough that the rainbows of our life would never perish,
Thank You

35. Meltdown

Ages to come and go, an iceberg does not sink.
Majestic it remains, you and I think.
The temperature does not drop for a while,
And it so strives to be for one more mile.

36. Know What You Are Building

You live in what you build...
A broken boundary or an opaque wall...
A high raised ceiling or an open sky....
Amidst the green meadows or on the rocky terrain...
You still live within what you build.

37. Fate and Candles

Every man who failed to light a candle would blame it upon the 'fate' he had never met.

38. The Universe to Live

You're the tranquility in the background of chaos,
A melody in the drop of dead silence, a ripple in the stagnant lake, a lightning in the bland sky.
Sometimes, even a dot in an entire spiral. Just that, for all of it, the universe has to continue to live.

39. Moon and the Ocean

The moon would once in a while reveal his face as a whole and the oceans would rise up to have a glimpse. The moon would then turn its face away, calming the ocean for the next few days. The cycle still repeats and the ocean believes that its never known the moon enough.

40. Tsunami and People

Some people are like a Tsunami Wave. You never know what they are capable of or how majestic they are until and unless they hit the shore.

Printed by Libri Plureos GmbH in Hamburg,
Germany

9 798888 833544